MW01618318

A Filipino Home

LITTLE FOLKS OF MANY LANDS

by

Lulu Maude Chance

YESTERDAY'S CLASSICS

ITHACA, NEW YORK

This edition, first published in 2025 by Yesterday's Classics, an imprint of Yesterday's Classics, LLC, is an unabridged republication of the text originally published by Ginn & Company in 1904. For the complete listing of the books that are published by Yesterday's Classics, please visit www.yesterdaysclassics.com. Yesterday's Classics is the publishing arm of Gateway to the Classics which presents the complete text of hundreds of classic books for children at www.gatewaytotheclassics.com.

ISBN: 978-1-63334-057-2

Yesterday's Classics, LLC
PO Box 339
Ithaca, NY 14851

PREFACE

CHILDREN delight in stories. They are interested in little folks of other lands. Teachers of to-day are alive to this fact.

Many devices are used in the schoolroom. Dolls are dressed in national costumes, pictures are collected, and special days are set aside for imaginary trips to foreign lands.

The stories in this book deal with race types. Not only are glimpses of home life given, but some of the folklore or hearthstone stories are here retold.

The chapters in this book have been a guide to one teacher, and it is hoped they may be to others.

CONTENTS

Yaba

LITTLE FOLKS OF MANY LANDS

YABA

YABA is a little Indian. She lives on a high hill. This has been the home of her people for many years.

Her tribe did not like to go to war. So they made their home on this hill. Here they were safe.

Yaba has red-brown skin. Her hair and eyes are black.

When she is older she will wear her hair in two large puffs above her ears.

Her mother's hair hangs down each side of her face. She winds it with cloth.

Yaba's dress is made of wool. It is one wide piece. She wears it over one arm and under the other.

When she is cold she wears a blanket. She has nothing on her head.

The men of this tribe weave the cloth. The women help to build the houses.

Yaba likes beads and rings. Her father makes them for her. He likes to wear them, too.

Let us go to Yaba's home. We climb far up to the top of the hill. The path is steep.

Here is the home of the tribe. It is one great house with many rooms. This house is made of stone and sun-dried brick.

Yaba's family live in one of the rooms. Her friends live in the others.

There are flat roofs on the rooms. Yaba's people sit here and talk, or watch the games on the ground below.

Yaba's brother runs in the races. She likes to see him win.

There are not many doors or windows in this great house. We see no steps to the rooms above.

Yaba shows us ladders. They can be moved from place to place. She tells us that these are the steps.

Women and girls carry the jars of water up the ladders. These jars are made of clay. The water is carried from the springs below.

Some Indians live in wigwams. Others live in huts made of brush. These Indians often move. They are not of Yaba's tribe. Her home is never moved.

We climb the ladder and go into the room with Yaba.

Here is a small fireplace. It heats the room in winter.

There are jars on the floor. Blankets hang from pegs on the wall. Bows and arrows hang from other pegs.

Now it is mealtime. A bowl of food is set on the floor. These Indians take up the food with their fingers.

Yaba is glad when the corn and fruit are ripe. Then her people have many feasts.

The Indians have songs and stories. The men sing of brave deeds. The women sing to the babies.

Yaba and her brothers like to sit in front of the fire and hear stories of the tribe. They learn the stories word by word.

The children like to hear the story of

TIYO, A LITTLE INDIAN BOY

He saw the river run past his home. It never came back. He set out to see why.

His father gave him a box of eagle's feathers. He must give these to the spider woman. Then she would show him the way.

He went to her house. She gave him a charm. This was to drive away the great snake and wild beasts.

Then the tiny spider woman sat on his ear. No one could see her.

She threw the feathers on the water and told him to follow them.

He went to the place where the sun rises. The sun took him round the world.

Tiyo saw the rain cloud. He wished to take it to his own home, but he did not know how; so he went to the home of the snake men.

They told him how to bring the rain cloud. He must paint his body and sing.

Tiyo did as he was told. Then the cloud came with its rain, and Tiyo's tribe was happy.

* * * * *

The Indians all like to watch the dances. The men paint their bodies and put on feathers. They sing and shake rattles as they dance.

They dance for rain, for good harvests, and for other things. They have a corn dance, a sun dance, and a snake dance.

Yaba and her brothers play games, but they have few toys. The boys have bows and arrows. They learn to shoot when they are very small.

There are steep paths over the rocks. The children climb and run on them.

They have great fun when the rain comes. Then the holes in the rocks are filled with water.

The children play in the small pools. They swim and splash in the water. When the long, dry time comes they often wish for the rain.

Yaba helps her mother grind the corn. They use two stones. The little girl sits on the floor while she works.

They make bread out of the meal. A fire is made under a flat stone. Then the thin sheets of bread are soon baked.

Yaba often burns her fingers trying to bake on the hot stone.

She helps to make jars out of clay. When she is older she will weave baskets and trays.

The men teach the boys to hunt and to work in the fields. Yaba's brother tends the sheep and cattle.

At the foot of the hill is a green valley. Here the Indians raise grain and fruit.

Yaba and her playmates have a little donkey. His Indian name means *big ears*.

The children like to play with Big Ears. They run races when they can make him go. If he does not wish to race he will not run.

Big Ears likes the children. Three or four often ride on his back at the same time.

The little donkey often climbs steep paths with large loads on his back.

Sometimes Big Ears is found in the field eating corn. Then the Indians cut off part of one ear. Now all who see him know he has taken corn.

These children have eagles for pets. The boys catch them when they are small. Here is a story of

AN INDIAN BOY AND AN EAGLE

One day the boy was out hunting with his bow and arrows. He found a young eagle. It had a broken wing and could not fly.

The boy took the bird in his arms. The eagle did not strike him with its beak but lay very still.

The little Indian took the bird home. He bound the broken wing with strips of skin. Then he made a soft bed of grass and leaves for it.

He fed the bird till the wing was well.

The bird grew day by day. It was strong again and must be set free.

The boy carried it to the rocks where he had found it. Here he set it free.

The Indian boy felt sad to part with his friend. He turned to go home. But the eagle flew over him and would not leave.

At last the boy hid in the trunk of an old tree. He was afraid some harm would come to his pet if he took it back home. He stayed in the tree till the eagle flew away.

Months went by but he did not forget the eagle. One day the boy was on the river in a bark canoe. He did not know he was near the great falls. When he saw the swift water he tried to turn his canoe. But the paddle broke.

Just then he saw an eagle flying to him. It came lower and lower. Soon it was over his head. It was his old friend.

The boy stood up in the canoe. He put out his arms and took hold of the eagle's legs.

The great bird flew upward with the boy and carried him safe to the shore. Then he spread his wings and flew away.

* * * * *

Indian boys have many dogs. These dogs climb ladders and lie in shady corners. They go with the boys to scare the crow from the fields. This story is told about a

WOLF AND SOME CROWS

A little wolf was passing a large tree. Some crows were dancing under it.

He stopped to watch them. They were in a ring and each crow had a bag on his back.

"What are you doing?" asked the little wolf.

"We are dancing with our mothers," the crows said.

"May I dance, too?" asked the wolf.

"If you will do as we tell you we will be glad to have you," said the crows.

The little wolf said he would gladly do as they told him.

"Then put your mother in a bag and come to the dance," they said.

Off ran the happy little wolf to get her.

He found the mother wolf at home by the fireside. He put her in a bag.

Then the sly little wolf went to the tree and began to dance with the crows.

At last one old crow said, "What did you bring in your bag?"

"My mother, as you told me," said the little wolf.

"Caw! caw! caw!" sang the crows. "Our bags are filled with sand," and they all threw the bags on the ground.

The little wolf was angry and ran home. He said he would kill and eat crows as long as he lived. And he has done so to. this day.

* * * * *

This is Yaba's baby sister. She is carried in a blanket on her mother's back. The blanket is small and is made just for the baby.

Now the mother has work to do, so Yaba takes the baby on her back.

Here we will leave our little friend on the high hill. She bids us good-by as we walk down the steep path.

Ikwa

IKWA

HERE is Ikwa. He is a little Eskimo boy. He lives in a cold land. It is far north of us. Let us visit him.

In summer the days are very long. In winter the nights are very long.

It is so cold here that trees cannot live. Only a kind of moss grows under the snow. It is brown and hard.

Eskimos burn the moss in oil to heat and light the huts. This is the only stove and lamp they have.

People in this cold land do not grow very tall. Ikwa is small for a boy of ten years.

His skin is yellow. He has bright black eyes. When he smiles he shows his white teeth.

Ikwa does not wash his face in water. He puts oil on it. This makes his face shine.

He must wear warm clothes; so he puts on two suits of fur. The inner one has the fur next the body. He wears the other one with the fur outside.

Eskimos are very brave. Ikwa's father hunts the bear and the seal. He uses the flesh for food. Clothing is made out of the skins.

Ikwa's mother makes his clothes. His jacket has a hood. When he is cold he puts the hood over his head.

His stockings are made from the skins of birds, with the soft down inside. Over these stockings he has boots of sealskin.

Ikwa's mother has two hoods on her jacket. Baby Mertuk is in one of them. She does not need warm clothes, for the hood is lined with soft down.

Ikwa's father is building a new house. He calls it an igloo. Let us watch him make it.

First he makes a ring in the snow. This is as large as he wishes the house.

On this ring he places blocks of snow. Then he lays more blocks on top of these. Each row leans a little more to the center than the row below. At last the house is built.

Ikwa and his brothers help now. They cover the igloo with snow. The shovels they use are made of bone.

Sometimes they throw the snow over each other. Then how they laugh and run!

There is only one room in Ikwa's home. A small hallway keeps out the wind and cold.

The window is a small hole over the door. There is no glass in it. The Eskimos cover it with a thin skin.

Let us go into the igloo. The door is low.

We must creep on our hands and knees. Now we can stand and look around us.

Ikwa takes off his outer suit. He does not wear it in the room.

We can see no table, bed, or chairs. Where do these people eat, sleep, and sit?

Ikwa tells us that the long bench by the wall is the bed. It is made of snow, with furs on it. The Eskimos sit on it, too.

Ikwa shows us the stove. It looks like a large shell and is filled with oil. Wicks of moss are burning in it.

This is the only kind of stove these people have ever seen. It lights the igloo and cooks the food.

Ikwa does not ask us to eat. His people eat only when they are hungry.

In summer the Eskimos often live in tents. These are made of skins.

This little boy and his playmates never saw a horse or a cow. They never ate fruit or candy. But they have something they like as well as we like candy.

Many birds come to this land in summer. Their feet and legs are red.

Ikwa's father kills some of the birds. His mother takes the bones out of their feet and legs and fills them with fat. This is their kind of candy.

Eskimos have dogs to draw the sleds. These dogs have small, sharp ears. Bushy tails curl over their backs.

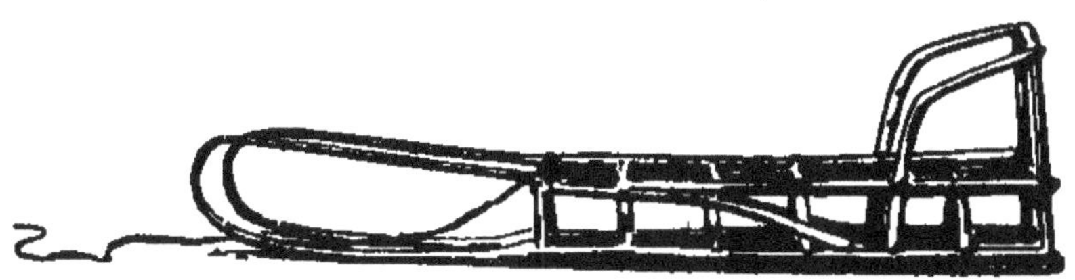

Six or more dogs often draw one sled. The harness is made of strips of skin.

The driver has a long whip, but he has no lines. When he drives the dogs he speaks to the leader. The other dogs follow this one.

Let us take a ride on Ikwa's sled. It is made of bones tied with strips of skin. He drives the dogs for us.

Ikwa snaps his whip and away we go. How the snow flies and how fast our dogs run! We must hold on to the sled.

Once Ikwa and his little sister were

riding on his sled. He drove the dogs far out on the ice. The dogs were going fast and the children were happy.

All at once they heard a loud crash. The great block of ice they were on had broken off from the rest.

The ice began to float from the shore out into the sea. Ikwa knew they might never see their home again.

As the hours passed it grew very cold. The little sister began to cry. Ikwa made a snow house to keep off the cold wind. He wrapped the warm robes from the sled about them. When the dogs whined he petted them.

It grew dark. Ikwa sat by his sister and watched all the night long.

The next morning the wind blew the ice nearer the shore. This made Ikwa very glad.

He saw some men on the shore. He called to them for help. They heard him and got into their boats.

The children must cross many blocks of ice to reach the clear water. Ikwa took his little sister by the hand. They jumped from block to block, slipping and falling as they went.

At last they reached the clear water. But the men could not come close to the moving ice with their boats. The waves were too high.

The men told Ikwa to throw his little sister to them. He threw her safely into a boat. Then he jumped into one. The dogs swam ashore and soon all were safe at home.

This little Eskimo boy has a long boat. He can paddle very fast in it. He likes to go with his father to fish.

Ikwa's father is going to hunt a seal. He cuts a hole in the ice. Then he sits down and waits.

Hours pass before a seal comes to this hole for air. The father spears it and takes it home.

Now the work begins. Every one helps. The father skins the seal. Then the people have a feast. The dogs have a share, too.

The mother and girls scrape the skin with bone knives. All the flesh must be taken off. Then the skin is beaten till it is soft.

Ikwa's sister helps the mother make shoes and clothes. The needles are made of bone. They use thin strips of skin for the thread.

These children of the north do not have many toys. When Ikwa was a small boy his first toy was a bow and arrow.

He liked to sit on the snow bed and aim at things in the room. One day a dog looked in at the low door. The little boy hit him on the nose with an arrow.

This was great fun for Ikwa. But

the dog did not like it. He growled and walked away.

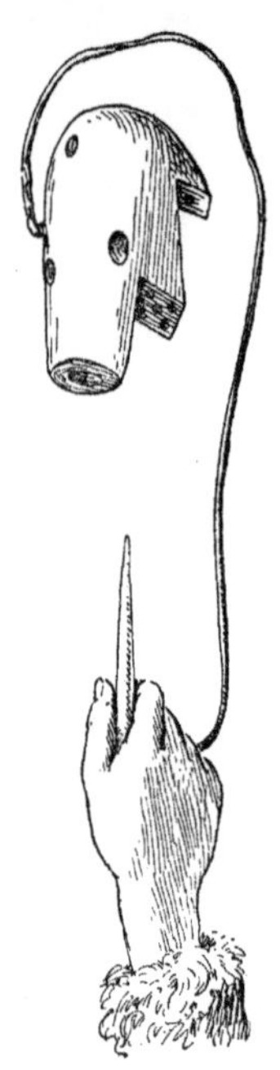

The children play with a pin-and-cup ball made of bone. One piece is sharp like a pencil. The other is much larger and has many holes in it. This is tied to the sharp piece by a strip of skin. Ikwa plays the game in this way. He holds the small piece of bone in his hand. He tosses the other up and tries to catch it on the small piece. If he misses, it gives him a sharp rap on the thumb.

The children like to play with the puppies. The boys train them to draw small sleds. This is not easy to do.

Sometimes the puppies upset the sleds. Then they run away as fast as they can go. At other times they sit down and will not move.

The Eskimo boys feed the large dogs and hitch them to the sleds. On long trips the dogs can go many days without food.

Ikwa and his friends like to play in the snow. They all stand in a ring. A ball is placed in the center. They cover it with snow.

The boys have long whips. They try in turn to hit the ball under the snow. They jump and shout when a boy strikes the ball.

Sometimes they put their heads between their knees and roll down hill. This makes them look like great snowballs.

One day the boys were playing in the snow. They saw a great white bear. He was coming as fast as he could run.

They cried for help and ran to the igloos. The men came with spears and killed him. After that they looked out for bears.

Ikwa's sister has a doll. It is made of sealskin. The eyes, nose, and mouth are made of beads. It has a fur suit with a little jacket.

Eskimo children cannot read. They have no books. But they have many stories. These are very old. They have been told many times. Ikwa's father heard them when he was a boy.

The story-teller turns his face to the wall. Then he tells the story slowly. The little children sit behind him and listen. The wick of moss burns in the lamp. It makes a dim light.

Let us leave Ikwa and his sisters with the old story-teller in their snow house.

Mina

Mina

MINA lives in Holland. People in her land are called Dutch. So Mina is a little Dutch girl.

She has blue eyes and rosy cheeks. Her hair is golden.

Mina looks like a little woman, for her dress is like her mother's. She has a long skirt and an apron. She wears a white cap every day.

There is a gold button on each side of it. Sometimes she wears a hat on this white cap.

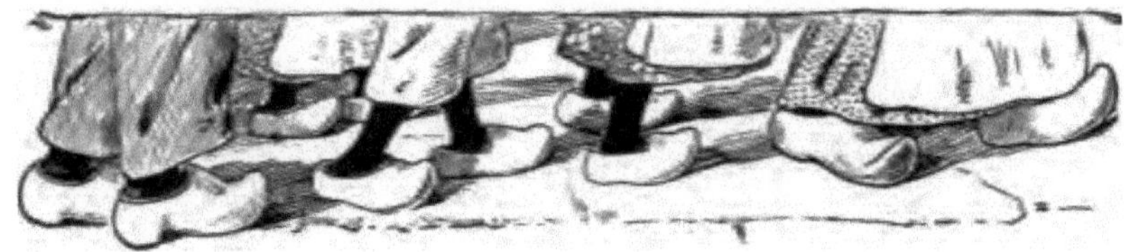

Mina's shoes are made of wood. When she walks they go click-clack.

The children wash their shoes with soap and water. This makes them clean and white.

These hard shoes do not hurt Mina's feet, for she wears thick stockings. She knits them herself.

Parts of Holland are lower than the sea. So the people have made great walls to keep out the water.

These walls are called dikes. They are so wide that roads can be built on them.

When there is a leak in the dike it must be stopped at once. The little leak would soon make a large hole. Then the sea would flow over the land.

It might drown many people. The houses would be washed away.

Every Dutch boy knows the story of

BRAVE LITTLE HANS

He lived many years ago. One day his mother sent him to the house of a friend. The little boy stopped to pick flowers.

The sun was low and it would soon be dark. Hans knew that he must hurry.

As he passed the dike he heard the sound of running water. He looked down and saw a small hole in the dike.

He knew it must be stopped or the great sea would soon cover the land. Hans ran to the place and put his arm into the hole.

He cried for help, but no one came. When it grew dark his people missed him. They went to find him. They hunted all night long.

At last the father heard a faint cry. There was the brave boy still holding back the great sea.

He was very weak and his arm was stiff and cold, but he had saved their homes.

* * * * *

There are many canals in Holland. Bridges are built over them. When a boat comes along the bridges are raised.

Let us watch the boats as they pass.

Some carry hay, fruit, and cattle. Others carry butter, cheese, and fish.

Here is a boat with a small house on it. We can see plants in the window and birds in a cage.

People live on these boats. They eat and sleep here.

There are many windmills in this country. They have great arms like sails.

The wind makes these arms go round and round. They turn wheels that grind flour and saw wood. They pump water from the low lands into canals.

Let us go with Mina to her home. As we walk along we see dogs drawing a cart. It is filled with cans of milk which a girl is selling.

We think it strange to see dogs working. The girl often lets them rest.

Here are children playing by the canal. What a clatter their wooden shoes make! Some of the boys are sailing shoes on the water for boats.

This little girl has a doll in a shoe. Another is playing with a tiny windmill.

Here are girls jumping rope in their wooden shoes. These boys are playing marbles.

One little girl has a stocking in her hand. She is knitting as she watches the others at play.

Here we are at Mina's home. We will leave our shoes at the door. Mina shows

us her mother's blue-and-white dishes, with canals and windmills on them.

This large red ball is a cheese. These tubs are full of butter ready to be sold. Holland sends butter and cheese to other lands.

Many black-and-white cows feed on the grass and hay in this low country. They give rich milk from which the butter and cheese are made.

Here is a story of how little Redcap helped the farmer with his cows.

LITTLE REDCAP

Once a poor farmer worked hard for a living. His wife was ill and could not churn. So the farmer did it for her.

He could do this only at night. When the sun was up he had to work in the field.

He slept till midnight. Then he got up to make the fire and to churn.

He went into the milk-room. There he saw an odd little man sitting by the fireplace.

He was dressed in red from head to foot. His face and hands were green. His tall cap had a long red feather in it.

Redcap was half asleep. The noise made by the farmer's wooden shoes awoke him.

The farmer was afraid and ran from the room. He did not churn that night.

But Redcap was his good friend. In

the morning the farmer found that the butter was all made. There was more than ever before.

The wife was soon well, but little Redcap churned for them each night.

The farmer grew rich and kept many cows. He sold the butter and soon had a stocking filled with shining dollars.

Redcap now did all his work. He took care of the cows and worked in the fields.

As the farmer became rich he grew lazy. He would not work, and spent his money for useless things.

His little friend Redcap told him this was wrong. But he did not listen to him.

One day the farmer came home angry. He told Redcap he must work still harder for him.

Redcap looked sad and went slowly out of the house.

Soon the wife fell ill again. The shining dollars turned to coals. The cattle died and the farm was sold.

The farmer found too late that he had done wrong. He wished for his little friend more and more. But Redcap was never seen again.

* * * * *

There are many sheep on the green fields. They are tended by shepherds who knit as they watch.

Pretty flowers grow in Holland. There are roses, lilies, and bright tulips.

Mina and her playmates have gay times when winter comes. The water freezes in the ponds and canals. Then the skating begins.

Dutch children learn to skate when they are very small. They laugh and shout as they play games on the ice.

There are sleds of all kinds. Some are like swans and others are like large shells.

There are chairs on runners. They are pushed by men on skates. Horses with bells draw the large sleds.

In winter the children often skate to school.

This large bird flying over our heads is a stork. It has long legs and a sharp bill. It rests by standing on one leg.

The people like these birds. Sometimes they place wheels on the roofs for them. Here the storks build their nests.

They are not afraid to walk on the streets. No one hurts them. They like to wade in the water and catch frogs.

When there are little storks in the nests the children often sing this song:

> "Stork, stork, fly away,
> Stand not on one leg to-day.
> Thy dear mate sits in her nest
> With the little ones at rest."

Mina likes to hear this story of

KING STORK AND THE FROGS

These frogs lived in a pond. They asked for a king. A log was put in the water for them.

Then all the frogs came and sat around him. But King Log never moved or spoke.

The frogs did not like this, so they called a meeting.

One said with a croak, "King Log will not move or speak to us. It is so still in the pond it makes one sad. Let us ask for a new king."

This time a stork was sent to them. It was not so still now in the pond, for King Stork chased them and ate them one by one.

* * * * *

At Easter time the children go from house to house for Easter eggs. They carry green leaves on the ends of long sticks. They wave them as they go singing down the street.

The children color the eggs. Then they have merry times with them.

The best time of all for Mina is Christmas Eve. A large sheet is put on the floor. The children stand round it watching for Santa Claus.

All at once the door opens. A rain of sugar-plums falls upon their heads. Santa Claus has come.

He has a bag of presents for good children and a bunch of rods for bad ones.

After the presents are all given Santa Claus tells them to look for him again next year. Then he goes to visit other little boys and girls.

Mina's mother tells her this story of good old Santa Claus.

SANTA CLAUS

A poor man was about to lose his home. His little ones would be turned out in the cold. He did not know what to do.

One night he sat alone in his cold room. All at once a purse of gold fell into his lap. He ran to the window but could see no one.

The next night gold rattled down into the fireplace. Still he could find no one.

The next night he saw the door open very slowly. He ran quickly and saw good old Santa Claus just as he was throwing more gold.

* * * * *

Some children think Santa Clans comes on a white horse. The night before Christmas they fill their shoes with straw for him. Then they go to sleep and dream of the pretty things Santa Claus may leave them in the wooden shoes.

Osom

OSOM

OSOM is a little black boy. He lives in a hot country. His home is near a great forest.

He has no books. He never heard of a school. But he can hunt and fish.

He does not work so hard as his sister. Minko helps her mother in the house and garden.

She sweeps the floor with a bunch of twigs. She carries wood and water.

Osom's mother hoes the corn in the

garden. She carries heavy loads in a basket on her back. When Minko is older she will carry one.

The mothers are very fond of the little girls. But the fathers like the boys better.

The men in Osom's country often go to war. They look very fierce when they are ready for battle.

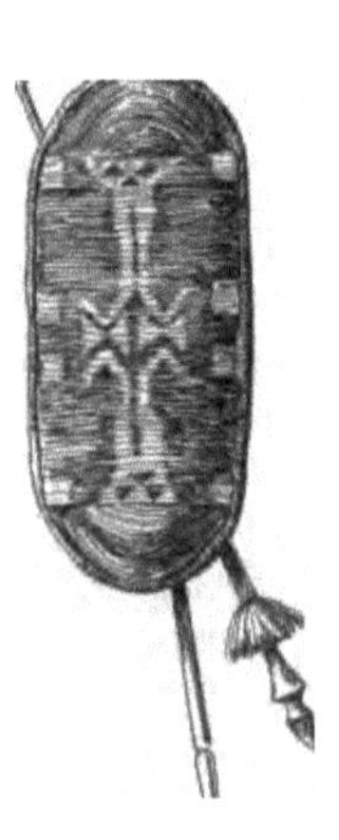

They hold shields in front of them and carry long spears and sharp knives.

The boys have bows and arrows. They learn to shoot with them when they are small.

These people are fond of music and dancing. They dance by stamping their feet on the ground. They move their bodies to and fro and swing their arms in time to the music.

They have drums, whistles, and rattles. Some dance while others sit on the ground and beat the drums.

The baby has a strange cradle. It is only a strip of cloth over his mother's shoulder.

He sits on her hip while she carries the heavy loads of wood.

Sometimes she puts him in the basket on her back. Then only the top of his little woolly head can be seen.

Osom lives in a hut made of grass and bark. The roof is made of palm leaves.

All around the hut are banana trees. Osom plays under them and eats the fruit. He chases the large butterflies that fly about.

There are many tribes of black people in Africa. They do not all build their huts in the same way.

Osom's house has no windows. There are two small doors. One is at the front of the house. The other is at the back.

Let us step inside. Here is a large stone. The women and girls grind corn on it.

The baskets which the women carry hang on the wall. The father's fishing net hangs there, too.

Here are some wooden spoons and a hoe. The bed is made of long poles placed side by side.

Osom's people have fruit to eat and good things from the garden. For a feast they eat roasted ants.

The father goes into the forest to hunt. The other men and the large boys go with him.

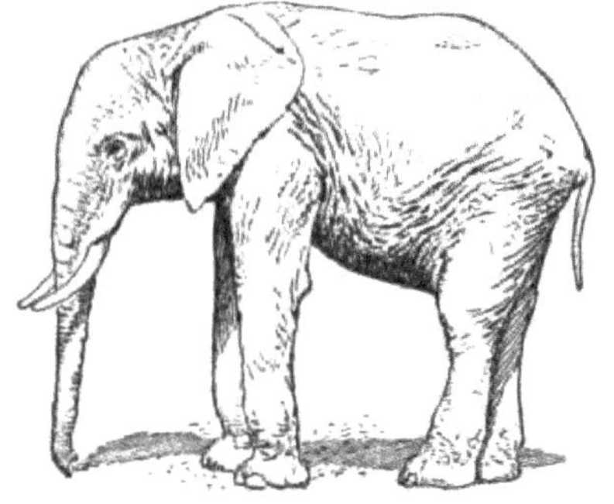

There are lions and other wild animals. Elephants are hunted for their tusks of ivory.

This animal is very large and strong. He has a long trunk.

When he takes a drink he fills his trunk with water. Then he pours the water into his mouth. If he wants a bath he pours the water over his back.

Men train elephants to work. They can carry heavy logs with their trunks.

Many kinds of monkeys chatter in the trees near Osom's home. Some are as tall as men. Others are so small that you could put one in your pocket.

They use their fore legs as arms. Their hands are very strong.

Some monkeys go far into the forest, jumping from tree to tree. An old monkey leads the way. The little one clings tightly to its mother's neck.

The mother swings with one hand on a branch. Then she jumps far out to catch hold of the next tree.

Parrots screech as they fly about. Osom's father sometimes brings one home.

There are strange trees in the forest. Vines grow over some of them. In the trees are many birds with bright feathers.

The men and boys are away for days on hunting trips. When they come home they bring ivory and rubber.

They trade these with the white men for beads and cloth.

Rubber is made from the sap of trees. These trees grow in hot countries. Some of them are in the forest near Osom's home.

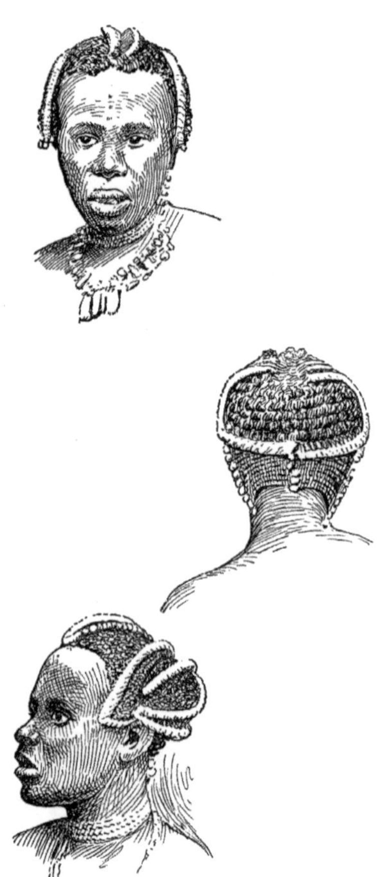

Let us see how rubber is made. This is one way.

A small cut is made in the bark of a rubber tree. Then under it. The sap flows slowly into this cup. When the cup is full it is taken away.

Now a fire is made. A stick is put into the sap and held in the smoke. The heat and smoke change the sap to rubber.

When you play with a rubber ball again think of what you have learned about it.

We have seen where Osom lives. Now let us see how he looks.

He has bright black eyes. His skin is black and his hair is woolly.

Look at the picture and see how his mother wears her hair. It is put over a small frame of bamboo. She wears beads and shells on it.

Most of Osom's hair has been cut off. Only a little is left on the top of his head.

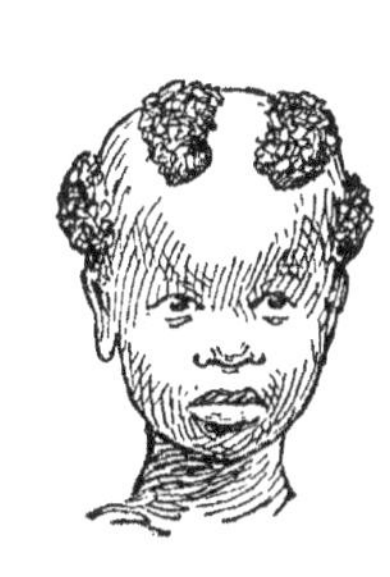

He wears a strip of cloth about his waist. He likes bright beads and rings.

Osom's mother wears heavy rings on her ankles. The girls and women have bracelets on their arms. Some of them reach from the hands to the elbows.

The men like to wear rows of monkeys' teeth round their necks.

These children have many games. The boys have more time for play than the girls.

Osom likes to roll a ball past a line of boys. Each one throws a spear and tries to hit the ball as it passes.

These boy's have many games with spears. They learn to throw them very far.

The children play "cat's cradle" with a string. In this game they can use their toes as well as their fingers.

The boys know where to find shells

with sharp points. They throw these at marks, as our boys throw tops at marbles.

The children like to hear stories of animals. Osom likes this one about

THE LION AND THE SNAKE

The lion said to the turtle one day, "I have caught all the animals in the forest but the snake. Will you catch him for me?"

"Yes," said the turtle; "go into the forest and I will catch him for you."

When the lion had gone the snake came. He said to the turtle, "I have caught all the animals in the forest but the lion. Will you catch him for me?"

"Yes," said the turtle; "go into the forest and I will catch him for you."

After the snake had gone the turtle dug a deep pit in the bushes near his home. He put grass and leaves over the top.

Soon the snake came crawling to him and said, "Where is the lion I asked you to catch for me?"

The turtle said in a low tone, "Don't speak. The lion is coming. Run and hide."

The snake crawled into the bushes. Crash! he went into the pit.

The turtle came near and said, "Sh! Keep still. The lion will hear you. You are in a safe place."

He put grass and leaves over the pit again. Then he sat near and waited.

Soon the lion came leaping over the grass. The turtle said to him, "Run, hide over there! The snake is coming."

The lion ran to hide and he, too, fell into the dark pit.

The snake said, "What's that?" And the lion said, "What's that?" But the turtle said, "Ha, ha! Now I have you both in the pit. Make the best of it."

Then they fought till the lion killed the snake and the snake killed the lion. The turtle threw bushes over both and left them in the pit.

Ahmed

AHMED

SEE this boy on a horse. How well he rides! It is Ahmed, a little Arab.

He is playing a game with his friends. They are all on horses. The boys are throwing spears as the horses run.

Arabs are very fond of horses. They make pets of them.

Once an Arab chief fell into the hands of robbers. They tied his hands and feet. His horse was tied near by.

In the night the horse got free. He picked up his master with his teeth and carried him to the far-off tent. There the weary horse dropped dead.

Arab children have been told this story many times.

In some parts of the desert there is no rain. In other parts it rains a little. Then the grass springs up. Here Ahmed's father finds grass for his horses and camels.

Many tribes on the desert live in tents. It is easy for them to move from place to place.

They must cross the hot, dry desert to reach the green spots. These people often travel at night under the bright stars. Then it is cooler.

There are sand storms in the desert. The wind blows hard and the air is very hot. The camels lie down and put their noses in the sand. Here they find cooler air to breathe.

In our country we travel by rail or by water. In Ahmed's country the people travel in caravans. These are trains of camels or horses. Let us watch them.

This camel has a heavy load. It is the tent in which Ahmed lives. Another camel carries the food. Another carries bags filled with water to drink. These bags are made of skins.

Here is a camel with a small tent on his back. It belongs to Ahmed's mother and sister.

The camel kneels for them to get inside the tent. Here they ride till the long trip is ended.

Here comes Ahmed's father. He has black eyes and hair. The sun has made his skin dark.

The father wears a black-and-white cloak. It is made of camel's hair. Over his head is a silk cloth. It hangs down on his shoulders.

Ahmed's mother is coming, too. She covers her head and dress with a cloak. Ahmed wears only a loose blue coat.

The camel has a hump on its back. Long hair grows on this hump. The neck and legs of the camel are very long. It has pretty brown eyes.

The camel is very useful to Ahmed's people. They drink its milk. They weave the hair into cloth for tents and clothes. Bags and baskets are made from its skin.

The camel can travel three or four days without drinking. Wide feet keep it from sinking in the sand.

This story is told of a donkey and a camel.

The donkey was once walking by

the side of a camel. The little animal fell down.

He said to the camel, "What keeps you from falling?" The camel said, "You look only as far as your nose. I look far ahead. Then I see the rocks and holes in my path."

Let us travel across the desert with Ahmed. We must start early, before the sun is hot.

Every one is busy. There are tents to take down and camels to load. The camels are lying on the ground. They are ready for their loads.

One old camel is very angry. He is making a great fuss. He thinks his load too heavy. His driver cannot make him get up.

He growls as he turns his head from side to side. When he does this the driver knows that some of the load must be taken off.

Ahmed is on his camel. So we will get on ours.

He kneels and we climb into the high seat. Ahmed tells us to hold on to the saddle. It is made of wood, with thick rugs on it.

We do as he tells us. Now we are ready for our camel to stand.

First he rises a little on his hind legs. This nearly throws us over his head. Then he rises on his fore legs and we almost tumble over his tail.

We feel sure we are going to fall. It does not seem so funny as it did at first.

The camel is up at last and we are glad. Ahmed laughs. He knows just which way to lean when his camel rises.

Now the caravan starts. Some of the men are on horses. Others are on camels.

When it is too hot to travel the tents are set up on the hot sands. We eat dates and drink camel's milk.

Here we rest and listen to stories. Ahmed's father tells this one of

THE ARAB AND THE CAMEL

An Arab sat in his tent. The night was cold. A camel stopped and looked in.

"Please, master," he said, "let me put my head in the tent. I am very cold out here."

"Of course," said the Arab. So the camel put his head inside the warm tent.

Soon he said, "May I not warm my neck also?" "Yes, indeed," said the Arab.

By and by the camel said, "It will take but little more room for my fore legs. May I not put them in?"

The good Arab moved aside and made room for him in the small tent.

"May I not come inside?" said the great animal at last. "I keep the tent open as I stand now."

"Yes, yes," said the Arab. "Come into the tent."

So the camel came inside. But the tent was too small for both of them.

"I see," said the camel, "that there is not room for both of us. It will be better for you to step outside. You are smaller than I. Then there will be plenty of room for me."

Saying this, the camel pushed the kind Arab out of the tent.

* * * * * * *

Now the air is cooler and we will start again.

We meet other caravans. The camels have loads of dates and ostrich feathers.

A strange bird lives in this country. It is an ostrich. It has a small head and long legs. It is as tall as a horse and can run very fast.

This bird has wings, but they are too

small for flying. Its feathers are long and soft. The ostrich lays its eggs in the sand. These eggs are so large that one of them makes a meal for three or four people.

Ahmed's father sometimes brings one home. The children think it a great treat. Now Ahmed is happy. He sees tall trees on the desert. He knows there is a grassy spot ahead. Here he will find sweet dates.

The horses and camels are glad, for they know that water is near. They like to eat the dates, too.

People could not travel over the desert if there were no green spots.

The date tree is one of the most useful trees in this land. It grows very tall. The leaves and fruit are near the top. Ahmed can climb this tree like a monkey.

The Arabs use every part of the date tree.

The trunk is made into posts. They weave the leaves into mats and baskets. The children think the fruit is the best of all.

The tents of the Arabs are not like the tents we have seen. They are low and flat. The cloth of the tent is made of camel's hair.

These Arabs sit on the floor to eat. The men eat first, and then the women and children. They all eat from a large bowl.

The women and girls grind wheat into flour between two stones. This flour is made into thin bread.

Ahmed does something that you cannot do. He eats his plate.

Let us see how he does it. His mother gives him some thin bread. He puts his meat on it. After he has eaten the meat he eats the plate, too.

The children have great fun with the little colts. They often keep them in the tents.

The boys must learn to throw spears and fire guns, for the Arabs often fight with other tribes.

These boys have many games. In one a boy is tied by his hand to a peg in the ground. He is at the end of a long rope.

The other boys have small whips. They run near and try to strike him.

If he can catch a boy, that one must be tied in his place.

Arab boys like the games with spears best of all. Then their fathers watch them.

The boys choose sides. Each boy throws a spear to the boy in front of him. This one must catch the spear in one hand and at the same time throw his spear back with the other hand.

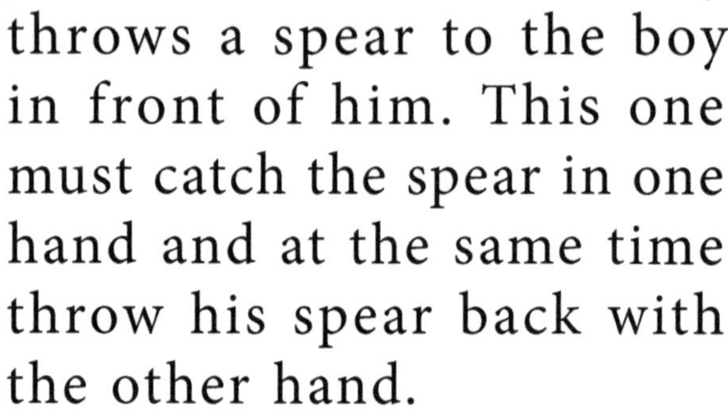

Arab boys who live in the towns go to school. They take off their shoes at the door, but keep on their hats.

They all sit on the floor and sway their bodies as they study aloud. The girls do not go to school.

Ahmed's sister helps her mother take care of the tent. She learns to weave cloth. She takes care of the little Arab baby, too. It lies wrapped in a cloth with its tiny arms at its sides.

Our trip is ended. It is time for us to leave our little friends of the desert. They say good-by to us at the door of their low tent.

Tona

Tona

TONA'S home is in a warm country. We must go halfway round the earth to reach it.

When the sun is over our heads it is night where she lives. She is fast asleep.

Tona is a little Filipino girl. She lives on an island. The water is all around it.

She has never seen the ground white with snow. In her land the grass is always green. Many pretty flowers bloom there. Some are as large as plates.

One kind has a leaf that looks like a cup. This leaf has a lid and will hold water.

Let us take a trip over the island. In the forests are monkeys and wild animals. Ferns grow as tall as trees.

There are many birds on the island. Some build strange nests. These nests are sold to the Chinese, who make soup of them. There are parrots and doves also.

The children like to hear the story of how the dove was once a child.

The child was playing in the hut. The mother would not give it a small rice cake she had just made.

The child was sad and ran from the hut. It made two wings out of palm leaves. Then it turned into a dove and flew away. The dove still cries for the rice cake.

Rice and sugar cane grow in this country. The children like to chew the fresh sugar cane. Boys and girls help in the rice fields.

Coffee is raised here. The plants have pretty white flowers. The coffee berries are picked when they are red.

Each berry has two seeds. They are the coffee beans.

These tall trees are coconut trees. They have large leaves near the top. In the leaves are clusters of coconuts.

The children like to eat these nuts. They drink the water that is found inside.

Tona's mother uses coconut oil in her lamp. She puts water in a bowl. Then she puts oil on the water and burns a wick in it. Sometimes the light burns all night.

Many kinds of fruit grow on this island. Some we have never seen.

Bananas grow around Tona's home. She likes to eat this fruit.

Out of little threads that grow in the pineapple leaves a thin cloth is made. Tona's mother weaves this cloth.

One of the most useful plants here is the hemp. Its fibers are made into ropes and cloth.

Tona's home is made of bamboo and matting. There are no nails in it.

The father makes a frame of bamboo. This is tied with strong vines. Then he hangs the walls of the house on it. These walls are made of woven mats. He covers the roof with palm leaves.

The house is built on poles above the ground. When it rains hard and the ground is wet the house is dry inside.

The steps are bamboo and so are the floors. These are made of poles tied side by side. When Tona walks on them they shake and creak.

The windows of this little girl's house are not made of glass. They are made of very thin shells. The windows have shades which are left open in the daytime.

Tona's people use the palm tree and bamboo for many things. They build houses, fences, and bridges of them.

The children have kites and other toys made of bamboo.

Filipino boys play many games with tops and kites. They like to see who can send his kite the highest.

Sometimes they have a battle with the kites. They tie sharp bits of shell on the strings. Then they try to cut the strings of the other kites and make them fall.

The boys play a game of football. One boy tosses the ball into the air. As it comes down he kicks it up again.

All the boys now run and kick the ball. They must keep it in the air by kicking it. They must not touch it with their hands.

Tona and the other little girls have their games, too. They play one with sticks of wood and two small stones.

They make a ring in the sand and place the sticks inside. Then they try to throw the stones so as to send the sticks out of the ring.

The children like to dive and swim. They learn when they are small. When they are in the water they must look out for sharks. These are large fish that eat people.

The Filipinos like music and have many bands. The children like to dance when the band plays.

Tona's mother tells her little ones this story.

THE JUNGLE BIRD

One day each year the jungle bird comes. The children in the street hear sweet music. It is the song of the jungle bird.

The children draw near. They see a flock of birds in a large ring. They are dancing and singing.

The little ones begin to dance and sing with them. The birds lead them deep into the forest. Then the sweet music stops. The birds scream and fly away.

The children are lost in the forest. This is the work of the jungle bird.

* * * * *

Tona's skin is brown. Her eyes are dark and her hair is straight and black.

Filipino girls dress like their mothers. Tona wears a loose jacket and a long skirt. She has no shoes or stockings.

But she often wears sandals. They have toe straps to keep them from falling off.

This little girl does not wear a hat. Her father has one made of bamboo. It is large and he can use it for an umbrella or a basket.

Tona's father goes out in the boat to fish with a large net. He salts and dries the fish.

This little girl has a pet monkey. He plays with the children. When he wants to eat a coconut he climbs a tree for it. There he chatters away and sometimes throws down a nut.

Tona helps her mother. She learns to weave mats and baskets.

She often carries wood to put in the stove. The stove is made of red clay. She sits in front of it and puts in a stick at a time to keep the fire going.

Tona often cooks rice on this stove. The people eat much rice in her country.

They chew a nut which makes their teeth and lips very red.

Let us take a walk with Tona near the river. On the water are two horns spread far apart. Under them are two black eyes and a nose. Tona tells us that a water buffalo is bathing.

He must go into the mud and water often or he cannot live. He plows the fields and does other work.

These animals are not cross if they can bathe. The children are not afraid to climb on their backs and take a ride.

Tona likes to watch the fireflies as they fly about at night. But she does not like the large bats that fly over her head.

She weaves a pretty basket for us. Her brother fills it with fruit and flowers. Then we climb into the little cart and go down to the great boat that is to take us home.

Matsu

MATSU

THIS is little Matsu. She lives in a land far over the sea. When Matsu was a baby she was often tied on her sister's back. Here she took her nap or watched the games with her bright eyes.

Her sister played hop-hop and bounce-the-ball. The baby had many a bump, but did not cry.

When Matsu was small her head was shaved. Only a little hair was left on the top. Now she is older and her hair is longer.

Matsu lives in Japan. Many of her little friends are named for trees and flowers. Her own name means pine tree.

Matsu's shoes are made of wood. She keeps them on by slipping her toes under the straps.

She often runs about in her stockings. They are not like yours. They have places for the big toes. If they were not made so, her shoes would fall off.

Matsu does not wear her shoes in the house. She leaves them at the door. Here she puts on sandals. They are made of straw and are very light.

Girls in Japan dress like their mothers. Matsu's dress looks like a long coat. She wears a sash with a large bow tied behind. The wide sleeves are her pockets. Here she carries her dolls and her books.

Our little friend does not wear a hat. When she is in the sun she holds a paper umbrella over her head.

Matsu's home is only one story high. It is made of bamboo. Let us go in.

Here comes Miss Pine-tree to meet us. She does not shake hands with us, but bows many times almost to the floor. This is her way of showing how glad she is to see us.

We sit on thick mats on the floor. It is a cold day, so a man brings a box of hot coals to warm our hands. This is the stove.

Small tables are now set in front of us, with bowls of rice. Matsu eats her rice with two small sticks. They are called chopsticks. They are made of ivory.

Two sticks are by the side of each bowl. We try to use them, but it takes a long time to get the rice to our mouths. It slips off the sticks.

All the people in Japan drink tea. Matsu brings our tea in pretty cups made near her home.

Now the tables are taken away and we play games and listen to stories. The little people of this land have many storybooks. They tell us this story about

AMA, THE SUN FAIRY

Ama was a fairy. Her home was in the sun. She had a brother who lived in the sea. The little sister was afraid of the waves.

They roared so loud she took her light and hid in the cave. This made the world grow dark.

Her brother went to the mouth of the cave and begged her to come out. But Ama would not come. She was still afraid.

At last he hid behind a rock. Then he held a bright glass before her. "This must be a strange fairy," said Ama. So she came out to talk to her.

Then her brother caught her. He carried her back to her home in the sun. "The waves shall not harm you," he said.

This made Ama happy. She still lives in the sun and shines for us all.

* * * * *

At last it is bedtime. The mother places thick quilts on the floor for us.

Here we will sleep. The bed is not hard, for the matting is thick.

But the pillow is not so soft. It is made of wood, with a pad of white paper on it. When we need a clean pillow, we take off a sheet of the paper.

The beds are ready and screens of bamboo and paper are drawn out to make our rooms. At first the pillows hurt our heads, but we are soon asleep.

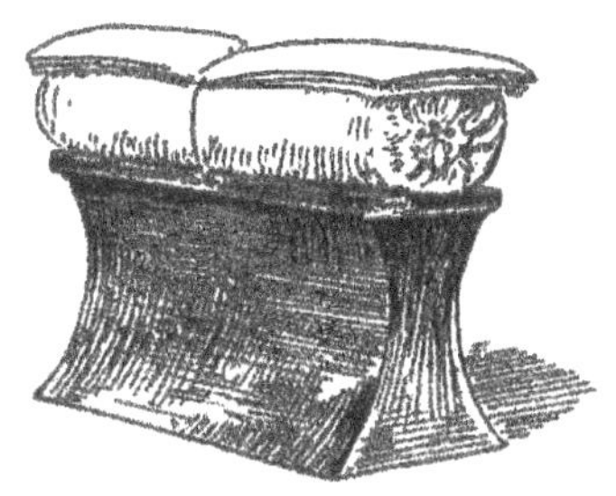

In the morning the screens are drawn back. In this way all the rooms are made into one large room. The quilts and pillows are put away in the closets.

Matsu comes to take us for a ride in an odd-looking cart. It is not large, and has two poles in front.

We step in and a man takes up the poles. He gives the cart a tilt that almost throws us out. But we cling to the sides and away we go. The man is strong and can run like a pony.

We see people working in mud and water.

Matsu says they are planting rice.

The rice seeds are planted in small beds. When the little plants grow they are set out in fields covered with water. The white seeds grow at the top of the stalk.

Now we are passing a tea field. It looks like a green garden. The tea plants are set in long rows.

When the leaves are ready the workers pick the tender green ones. The leaves are spread on mats to dry. Then the tea is put in boxes to be sold.

Let us stop at this house where silk is made. Here are many trays filled with leaves. The leaves come from the mulberry tree.

Hungry little worms are feeding on the leaves. These worms are hatched from the eggs of a moth. When they grow large they spin cocoons.

The cocoons are unwound and made into thread. This is woven into silk.

We buy silk, as well as tea and rice, from Japan.

Now we are off again. We pass many apple, peach, and plum trees. Here are cherry trees too, all in blossom.

Matsu and her friends have many picnics in these groves. They go to see the pretty blossoms. When they are tired of play they listen to stories. Here is one of

THE MONKEY AND THE CRAB

A monkey met a crab on the road. The monkey picked up a seed. The crab was eating a rice cake.

The monkey wanted it. He said, "Will you give me that cake for this seed?"

"Yes," said the crab. So he took the seed and planted it.

Soon it grew into a tall tree and was filled with fruit.

Then the crab asked the monkey to pick the fruit for him. The monkey

climbed the tree and ate the ripe fruit himself.

He threw the green fruit down on the back of the poor little crab.

When the crab's friends heard of this they went to war with the monkeys.

But the crabs were soon beaten. They went to their homes to make new plans. They asked the rice bowl, the bee, and the egg to come and help them.

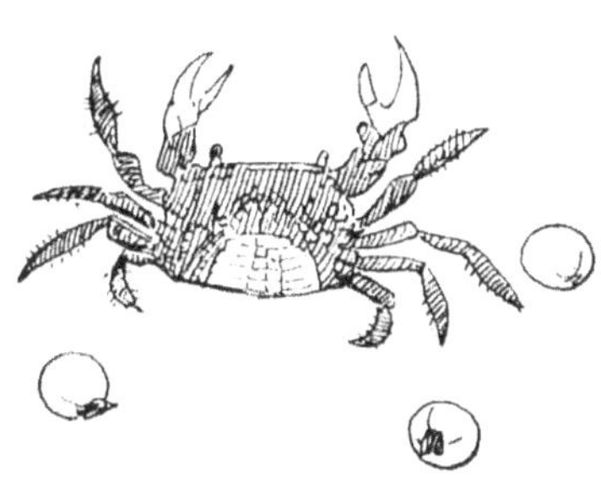

Then they went to the king of the monkeys. They asked him to meet with them and talk of peace.

The monkey came. He sat down by the fire. Bang! went the egg that was hidden in the ashes. The monkey's arm was burned.

He ran to a tub of water to stop the pain. The bee flew from behind the tub and stung him on the nose.

"Oh! oh! oh!" cried the monkey as he ran to the door.

Then the rice bowl fell and hit him on the back.

This made the monkey think of the poor crab whose back he had hurt. Then all the crabs rushed in and pinched him with their big claws.

* * * * *

Japan has many shops. In this one boys and girls are sitting on their heels. They are making lanterns. They bend bamboo into many shapes and cover it with paper.

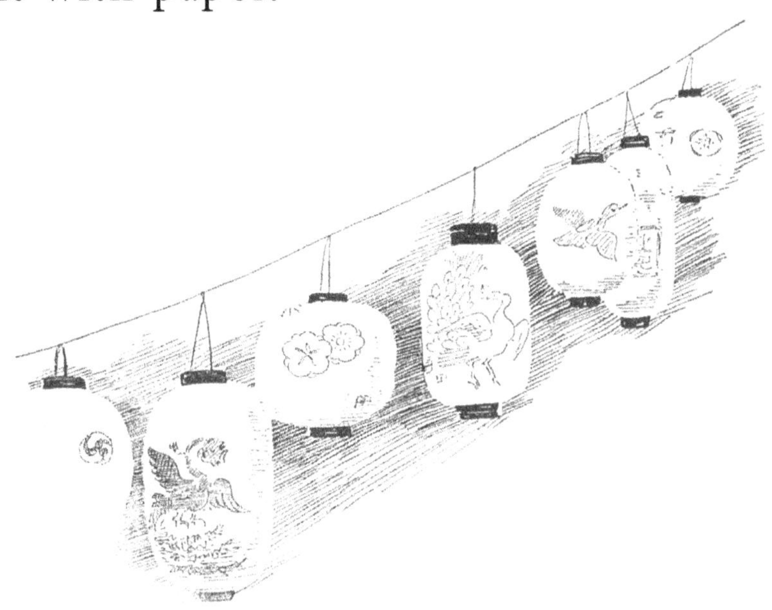

Fans and umbrellas are made in other shops. Many of these are sent to our country.

This man has toys to sell. He has drums, balls, tops, and butterflies made of paper. He makes animals of straw or bamboo.

Here is a man making toys out of paste.

The children watch him as he works. He makes dolls and funny animals.

There are many holidays in Japan. The first is New Year's day, but the games last many days. The children wear their best clothes. They give presents, as we do at Christmas.

At this time branches of bamboo and pine are hung on the gates. Flags and lanterns make the streets bright and gay.

There are many games. Matsu likes to play bat-the-ball with her playmates. They use light wooden bats. Some of the balls are large

seeds with feathers stuck into them.

Two or more girls play the game. They try to keep the ball in the air by hitting it with the bats.

There is a holiday for little girls. It is called the Feast of Dolls. It comes on the third of March.

All the shops have dolls. The happy children go from one shop to another to see them.

Matsu likes this day, for her mother takes out all the dolls in the house. There are Matsu's dolls, her mother's dolls, and her grandmother's dolls. They almost fill the room.

The little girls visit from house to house. They see the other dolls and have candy to eat.

When the day is over, some of the dolls are put away until the next year. Others are kept to play with. Matsu likes to tie dolls on her back, as she was tied when a baby.

The boys have a holiday of their own. It comes the fifth of May. Each boy has a paper fish in front of his

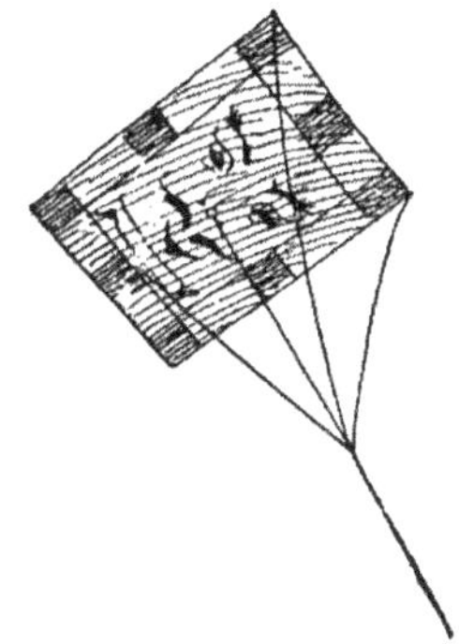

house. It is hollow, and the air makes it float and flap like a real one.

Matsu has one brother, so there is but one fish in front of her house.

The stores are filled with toys for the boys. There are bows and arrows, guns and soldiers.

Boys and girls in Japan like to play hide and seek and blindman's buff. They spin tops and fly kites.

The kites are of many shapes. Some are like birds and animals. Others have funny pictures painted on them. Many of the kites make a humming noise while flying.

Matsu does not play all the time. She helps

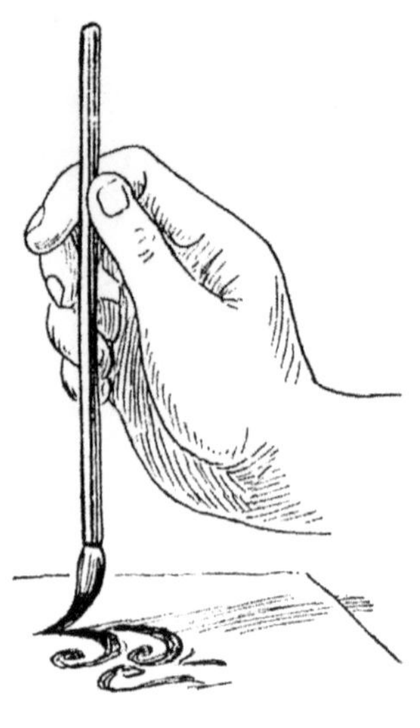

to sweep the floor and fold the beds. She can cook, sew, and make tea.

In school Matsu learns to write with a brush. She must hold her hand so that the brush will not blot the paper. This is the way she writes her name:—

Now the time has come to say good-by to Matsu. She bows many times to the floor and asks us to come again. We tell her how glad we shall be to have her visit us in our home.

www.ingramcontent.com/pod-product-compliance
Lightning Source LLC
LaVergne TN
LVHW050803210426
836822LV00013B/331

* 9 7 8 1 6 3 3 3 4 0 5 7 2 *